# Sea Fishing

## Tony Whieldon

**Introduction by Russ Symons**

**WARD LOCK LIMITED · LONDON**

First published in Great Britain in 1984
by Ward Lock Limited, 8 Clifford Street,
London W1X 1RB, an Egmont Company.

Reprinted 1986.

Printed and bound in Italy by
New Interlitho, Milan


**British Library Cataloguing in Publication Data**

Whieldon, Tony
    Sea fishing.—(Fishing skills)
    1. Saltwater fishing—Pictorial works
    I. Title      II. Series
    799.1'6      SH457

    ISBN 0-7063-6282-9

# Contents

**Acknowledgments**
My thanks to Michael, Graham and Bob, whose invaluable
assistance made the marathon a little shorter.

# Introduction

The sport of angling becomes more popular as leisure time increases, and there is little doubt that sea angling, with its multitude of attendant skills and abilities, is the fastest-growing section of this great sport.

Reasons for this fast-growing popularity are not difficult to find. It is a sport which gets people into the great outdoors, whether it be at sea in a boat, or on a beach or pier. It is also a sport which will stick with you through good times and bad. It can easily be made into a very expensive sport by the acquisition of a fabulous sea-going vessel equipped with the very latest in navigational, communication and fish-finding equipment; or it can be made to fit the slimmest of budgets by making the most of your own gear, digging your own bait and fishing from rocks, beaches or piers close to home.

Broadly speaking, sea angling can be divided into two categories, boat fishing and shore fishing, and they are two distinctly different branches of the sport.

The boat angler either owns a boat, or pays his share of a charter fee and fishes from a charter boat. These are usually run by a professional skipper whose livelihood depends on putting his clients over a spot which is known to hold fish. Charter boats vary considerably in size. There are small, inshore boats which rarely venture more than 10 or 12 miles from their home port. And at the other end of the scale there are boats equipped with a Decca navigational system, professional echo sounders, and so on.

These go 50 miles or more offshore to fish deepwater wrecks, often in water over 40 fathoms deep, in search of supersize pollack, cod, coalfish, or perhaps that ferocious denizen of the deep, the conger eel.

Boat anglers who own their boats are a breed apart. Not only do they have to know how to catch fish, but they must also be accomplished seamen, navigators, amateur shipwrights and mechanics – skills all too easily overlooked by the layman as he casually observes the angler unloading his catch.

Shore anglers also need to acquire skills not readily appreciated by the casual observer. These range from the delicate craft required to catch the grey ghost of inshore waters, the mullet, to the considerable athletic ability required to propel 5 oz (150 g) of lead some 100 yd or more, out behind the foaming surf.

There is another side to shore angling: often the best fish come from little-frequented beaches or headlands which sometimes require a hike of several miles, often over some rough terrain, so a good degree of physical fitness is required. And if you don't believe that, just try carrying a 30 or 40 lb (13.5 or 18 kg) pack half a mile along a shingle beach!

Newcomers to the sport often naively believe that if they buy the latest carbon fibre rod, a super reel, and all that goes with them, they are guaranteed to catch fish. Then they find that the veteran angler with his tatty old tackle can outfish them hands down. At this point the newcomer will either give up in disgust, or take his first step in learning what this great sport is all about, by confessing his ignorance to the veteran and asking his advice. Most times he will receive more help than he can assimilate, as well as an earbashing about how good it was in years gone by, but that is all part of the fishing scene.

From that moment, the fishing bug will begin to bite deep into your conscious life. You will discover that being an angler is more 'a way of life' than just a hobby, as it is so casually described by those who know no better. Your whole life will start to be governed by the state of the tide, wind and weather, to an extent beyond the comprehension of even your nearest and dearest. Those moments of minor triumph over the weekend will be with you through the week, giving rise to rumours among your workmates that you are a 'fishing nut'; but if you are one, you won't worry much about that.

It is recognized that in all sports, there is a hard core of knowledge, skills and physical abilities which must be learnt or developed in order to progress to genuine mastery and full realization of one's potential.

There are two levels of fishing knowledge: the overt kind, which can be learnt from books and evening classes; and the covert kind, which cannot be readily seen, and which can only be learnt through detailed observation and actual experience.

At some time or other we have all heard the tale of one angler catching fish, and another standing alongside him, using identical tackle and bait from the same bait box, who cannot catch a fish however hard he tries. This is a typical example of a covert skill. The first angler probably doesn't realize exactly what he is doing, he just knows that, whatever it is, it works.

Experience is the best teacher of any practical skill, and this is especially true of outdoor sports, particularly angling. You have to be out there in wind and weather, handling the boat, watching the compass and echo sounder, or prowling the beach or cliff top watching for nature's signs that the fish are feeding. A cloud of gulls wheeling and diving over the great green Atlantic rollers as the bass play in and out of them, cutting up the shoals of sandeels and britt; these scavengers give the game away by feeding on the debris as it floats to the surface. A crack-of-dawn stroll along the beach after a storm at sea will reveal the washed-up debris before the sea-shore scavengers destroy the evidence of what the fish are feeding on, out there behind the third breaker: perhaps a hermit crab, razorfish, scallop or crab. All are nature's clues, and should be acted upon, not next week, not tomorrow, but right at that instant. The fish will be there, looking for more tasty morsels.

This book doesn't hide what it says behind a hedge of words. Each picture is a statement which makes for clear and easy understanding, and forms a good base on which to build your practical experience.

Nice one Tony,

Russ Symons,
Plymouth, Devon

January 1984.

# Rods

BEACHCASTER:
 This rod is designed
to throw a bait a long
way. Distance is all
important if the fish
are feeding 100yd (27·8m)
plus from the shoreline.
 Lengths vary from 11ft
(3·50m) to 15ft (4·55m).

BOAT ROD:
 Boat rods are shorter
than beachcasters, 7ft
6in (2·30m) being about
the average length.
Some are equipped with
rings throughout, some
have rings with a roller
at the tip, and others
have rollers from tip to
butt.

SPINNING ROD:
 This is a useful
addition to any sea-
angler's armoury, for
casting a spinner or
float tackle. There are
many good hollow-glass
spinning rods to choose
from; solid glass rods
should be avoided.

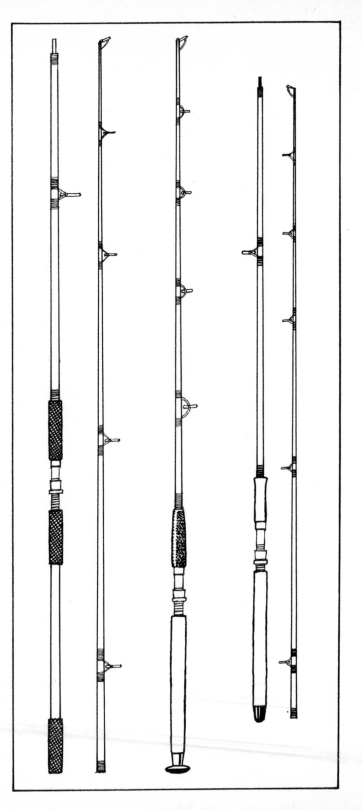

# Reels

FIXED SPOOL: This is the ideal reel for the beginner, providing trouble-free casting, and capable of casting a bait considerable distances. For maximum efficiency the reel should be loaded correctly; the procedure for doing this is shown on a later page.

BEACH MULTIPLIER: In the hands of an expert, this reel is second to none, both in distance-casting ability, and for providing direct and positive contact with the bait and fish. Here again, the reel's performance is affected if the spool is not correctly loaded.

BOAT MULTIPLIER: Unlike the beach multiplier, this type of reel is not designed for casting but for presenting a lure or bait beneath a boat. There are variations of this reel, some more suited to bottom fishing, and others to trolling. They also come in different sizes, from the smaller, light-line capacity to the large, big-game models. Manufacturers' catalogues supply detailed specifications.

# How to load a reel

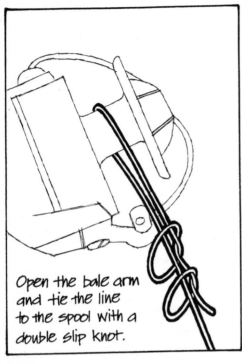

Open the bale arm and tie the line to the spool with a double slip knot.

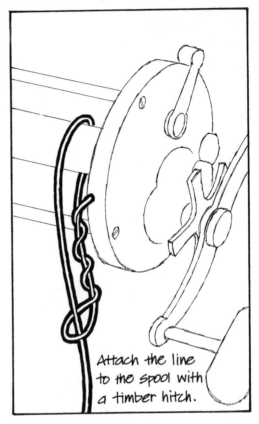

Attach the line to the spool with a timber hitch.

A correctly loaded reel.

Load to within ¼in (3mm) below the spool rim.

# Shock leader

This consists of 30ft (9·15m) of stronger line connected to the main line. Its function is to absorb the shock and stress of casting with a beachcaster. The breaking strain of the shock leader will depend on the weight of the lead. As a yardstick, if a weight of 6oz (180g) is being used, the breaking strain of the shock leader needs to be about 50lb (23kg). The shock leader should be attached to the main line correctly to ensure the knot does not foul on the rod rings during the cast.

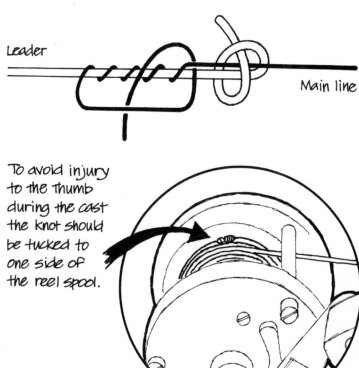

Leader    Main line

To avoid injury to the thumb during the cast the knot should be tucked to one side of the reel spool.

# Hooks

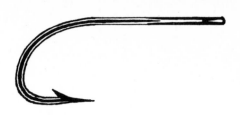

O'SHAUGHNESSY: An ideal hook for boat legering when fishing for conger and ling over rocky ground.

FINE WIRE ABERDEEN: This is the ideal hook for most light shore-fishing where the seabed is clean. It is the best hook for threading on a lugworm or ragworm bait, and is also ideal for livebaiting with a sandeel when boat fishing.

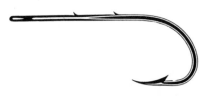

BAIT-HOLDER: This hook is very widely used, but the cuts in the shank probably do more harm than good by creating weak points.

FORGED STAINLESS STEEL: Where the seabed is rougher, or where large bass or cod are expected, this is the best hook for the job. In its larger sizes, eg., 7/0 or 8/0, it is capable of dealing with shore conger.

SEAMASTER: The `big daddy' of sea hooks. It is used in con-junction with a cable-laid wire trace, and is the only reliable hook to use for wreck conger, or shark. This hook ranges in size from 4/0 to a massive 16/0.

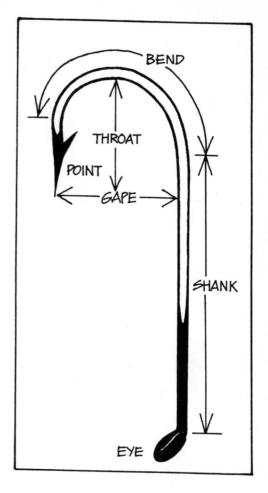

# Hook sizes and anatomy

4

2

1

1/0

2/0

3/0

4/0

5/0

6/0

7/0

BEND

THROAT

POINT

GAPE

SHANK

EYE

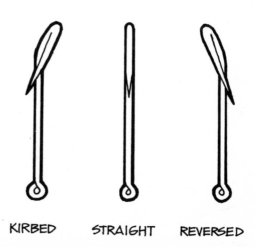

KIRBED          STRAIGHT          REVERSED

# Shore fishing leads

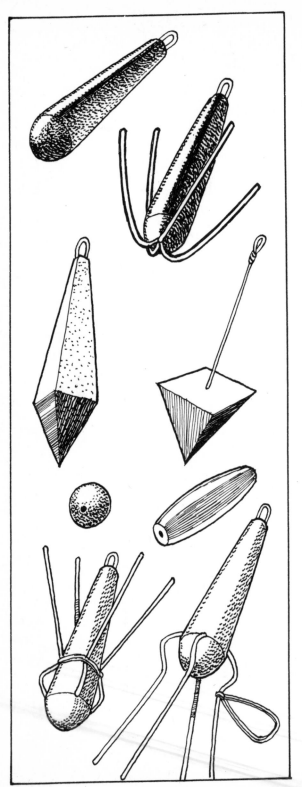

Casting bomb

Bomb with grip wires

Torpedo

Pyramid standfast

Drilled bullet

Barrel

'Breakaway' casting bomb

Closed                    Open

# Boat fishing leads

Some of the weights shown under the heading of shore-fishing can also be used for presenting a bait from a boat.

The drilled bullet, for example, is the best lead for keeping a live sandeel at the required depth.

Casting bombs can also be used in conjunction with a paternoster rig.

When trolling for bass over and around reefs, the spiral weight (shown opposite) is the number one choice.

Where a positive hold on the bottom is required, when legering in deep water with a strong tidal flow, the pyramid or grip lead should be used.

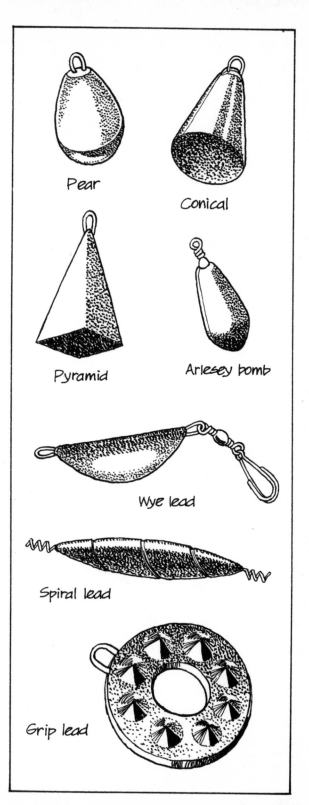

Pear

Conical

Pyramid

Arlesey bomb

Wye lead

Spiral lead

Grip lead

# Links and swivels

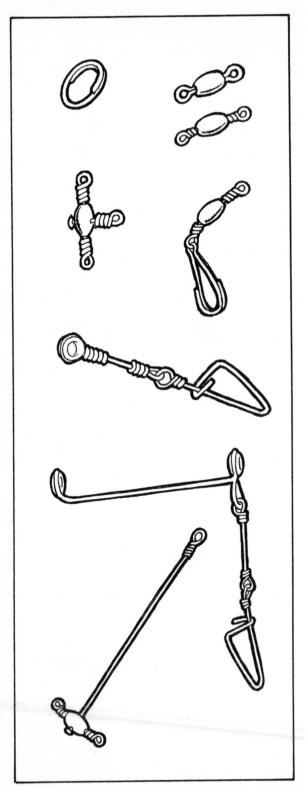

Split link

Barrel swivels

Three-way swivel

Link swivel

Kilmore link

Clement's boom

Three-way swivel boom

# Shore terminal tackle

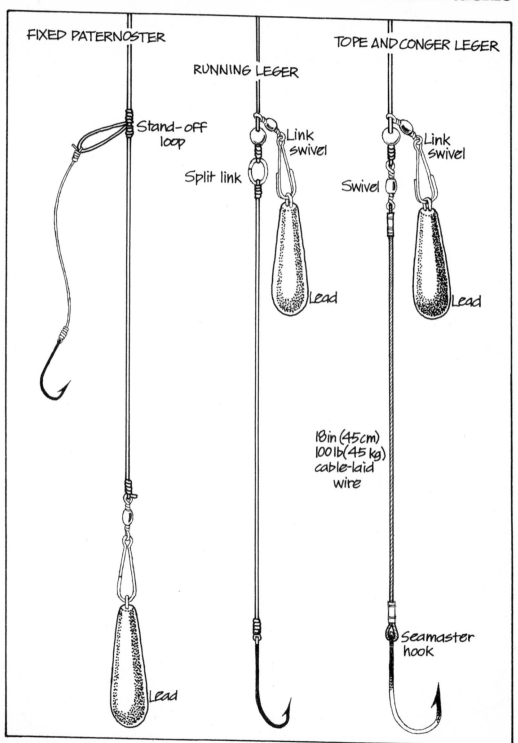

FIXED PATERNOSTER

Stand-off loop

RUNNING LEGER

Link swivel

Split link

Lead

TOPE AND CONGER LEGER

Link swivel

Swivel

Lead

18in (45cm) 100lb (45kg) cable-laid wire

Lead

Seamaster hook

Lead

# Boat terminal tackle

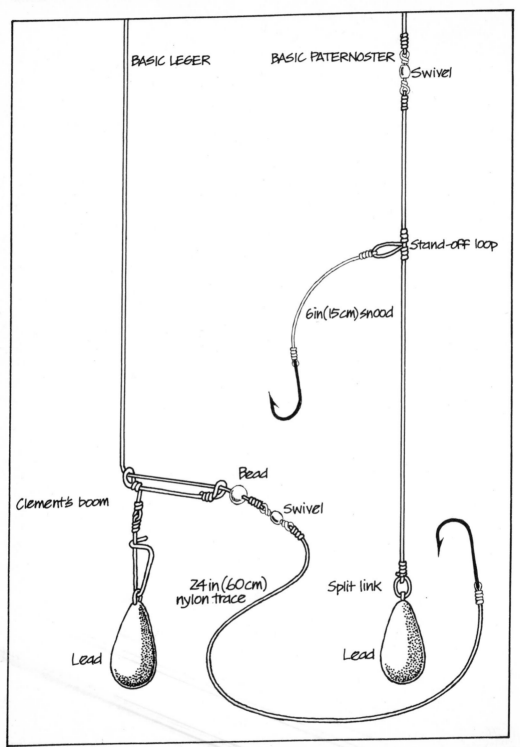

BASIC LEGER

BASIC PATERNOSTER

Swivel

Stand-off loop

6in(15cm)snood

Clement's boom

Bead

Swivel

24in(60cm)
nylon trace

Split link

Lead

Lead

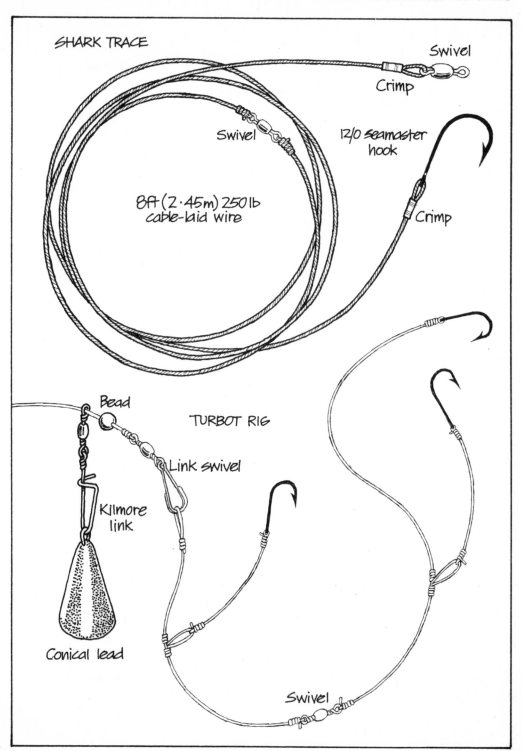

SHARK TRACE

Swivel

Crimp

Swivel

12/0 seamaster hook

8ft (2·45m) 250 lb cable-laid wire

Crimp

Bead

TURBOT RIG

Link swivel

Kilmore link

Conical lead

Swivel

# Boat terminal tackle

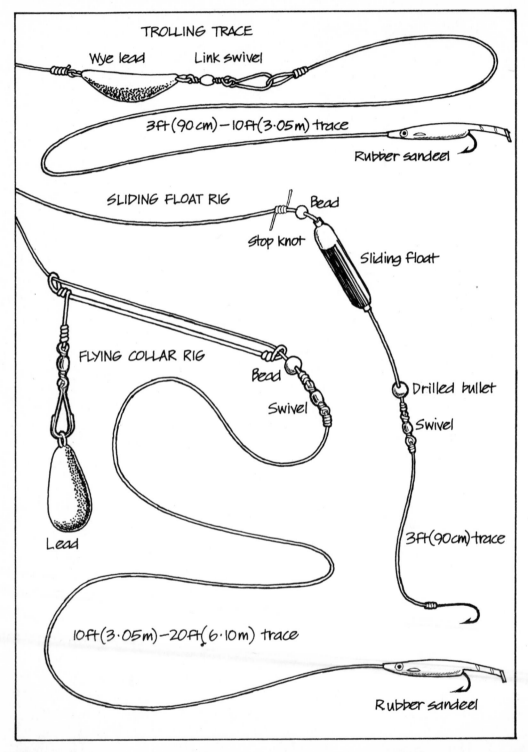

TROLLING TRACE

Wye lead          Link swivel

3ft (90 cm) – 10ft (3·05m) trace

Rubber sandeel

SLIDING FLOAT RIG          Bead

Stop knot

Sliding float

FLYING COLLAR RIG          Bead

Swivel

Drilled bullet

Swivel

3ft (90cm) trace

Lead

10ft (3·05m) – 20ft (6·10m) trace

Rubber sandeel

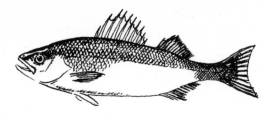

BASS Are found in greatest numbers in Atlantic coastal waters. They love to cruise around reefs, and often enter estuaries, where they follow the tide for many miles upstream.

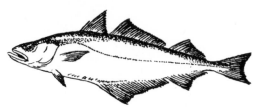

POLLACK A fish of rocks, reefs and wrecks. They are common all around the British Isles and the coast of Europe. Smaller pollack can even be found over a clean sandy bottom.

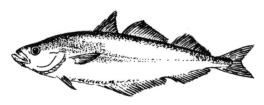

COALFISH Very similar to the pollack. The coalfish, however, has a straight, light-coloured lateral line, whilst the pollack has a dark lateral line with a kink near the shoulder.

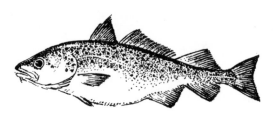

COD A fish that is widely distributed around Britain and Northern Europe. Offshore boat anglers can contact them all year round, but the shore angler has to wait for the colder months.

WHITING This greedy fish can be found just about anywhere during the winter months. It will grab both worm and fish bait, especially after dark.

POUTING Sometimes known as pout or bib, this ravenous little fish is probably more of a pest than any other fish that swims in the sea. Unfortunately it is very prolific.

# Species

HADDOCK  Not so widely distributed as the whiting, but common north of Biscay, where it is of great commercial value.

MACKEREL During the summer mackerel shoals harry small fry around the coasts of Britain and Europe. They will often drive the fry on to beaches, and will follow them well upstream in an estuary.

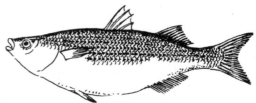

GREY MULLET  A fish of estuaries, lagoons, harbours and backwaters. They are also found all around the coastline, where they browse on weed.

BALLAN WRASSE This handsome fish is found only among rocks, and in water of a reasonable depth. It is mainly an Atlantic fish, but the North Sea has a few off the East coast of Scotland.

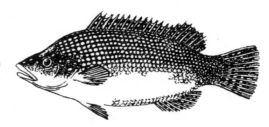

BLACK BREAM  A warm-water, summer visitor to northern European waters. It likes to shoal up around wrecks and rocky outcrops.

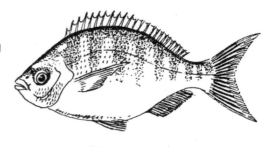

RED BREAM  Another summer visitor to northern European waters, but not as common as the black bream.

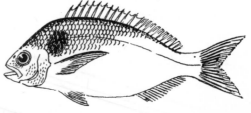

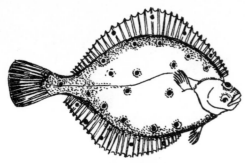

PLAICE Instantly recognizable by the large orange or red spots on the back. They will move in over sandbanks and mudbanks on a rising tide, where they feed on cockles, worms and crustaceans.

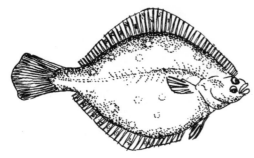

FLOUNDER This is a drab fish compared to the plaice. Some do have reddish spots, but these fade after the fish has been out of the water for some time.

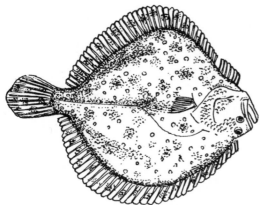

TURBOT This big predator lives on gravel, shell and sandy bottoms. It feeds heavily on other small fish, such as sandeels, sprats, herring, whiting and pout.

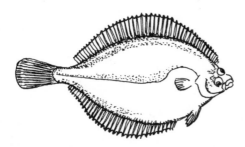

DAB A small flatfish, but what it lacks in size it makes up for in taste (the flesh is delicious). They prefer shallow water with a sandy bottom, and will provide non-stop sport for the angler who is lucky to fish such a place when the dabs are hungry.

# Species

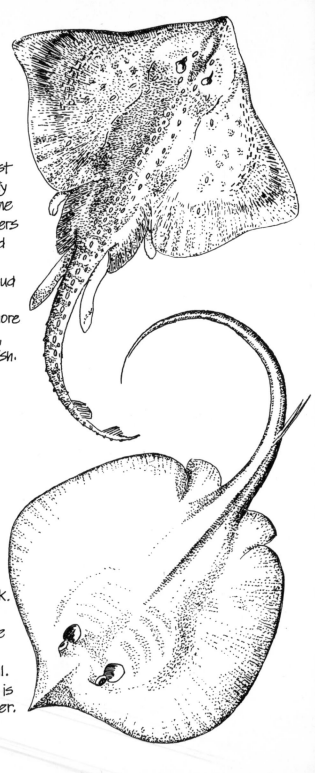

THORNBACK RAY  The commonest of all the rays. They are instantly recognizable by the spines along the back. They move into inshore waters with the arrival of spring and feed mainly over clear, sandy areas. Occasionally they will live over mud or gravel, but shun rocky areas completely. Their diet includes shore crabs, shrimps, sandeels, herrings, sprats, and various other small fish. It also goes under the name of 'roker' in some areas.

STINGRAY  A later visitor to inshore waters than the thornback. Food consists mainly of molluscs and crustaceans. The spine on the tail is venomous and any injury inflicted by it is extremely painful. Sometimes more than one spine is present, thus increasing the danger.

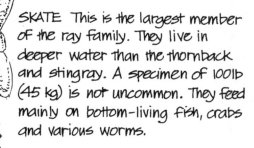

SKATE This is the largest member of the ray family. They live in deeper water than the thornback and stingray. A specimen of 100lb (45 kg) is not uncommon. They feed mainly on bottom-living fish, crabs and various worms.

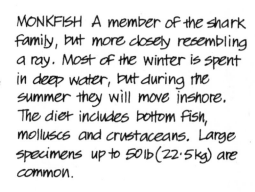

MONKFISH A member of the shark family, but more closely resembling a ray. Most of the winter is spent in deep water, but during the summer they will move inshore. The diet includes bottom fish, molluscs and crustaceans. Large specimens up to 50lb (22·5kg) are common.

## SPUR-DOG

A very common member of the shark family, with a venomous spine on each dorsal fin. They form large packs and hunt over a soft bottom, consuming sprats, sandeels, herring, garfish, bottom fish and crabs. The average weight is 14lb (6·3 kg).

LESSER-SPOTTED DOGFISH

Very common around the coast of Britain and Europe. They hunt over sand, gravel or mud, and feed on crabs, shrimps, molluscs and worms. The greater spotted dogfish, known also as nursehound, or bull huss, is less common than the lesser spotted variety, but, as the name implies, grows to a larger size.

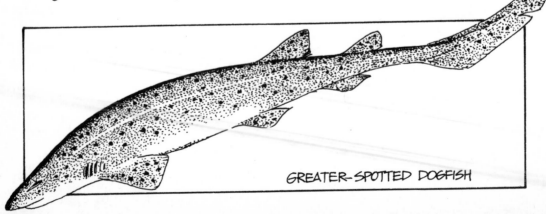

GREATER-SPOTTED DOGFISH

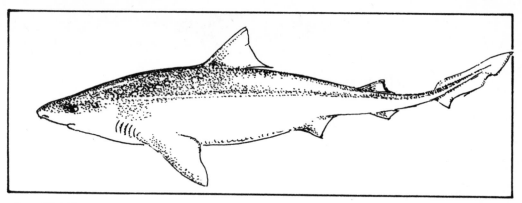

## SMOOTH HOUND

Two species of smooth hound are to be found in British and European waters: the common smooth hound, (Mustelus mustelus), and the starry smooth hound, (M. asterias). They live in comparatively shallow water near the shore-line where they feed on hermit crabs, other small crabs and lobsters. Bottom-feeding fish also form part of their diet.

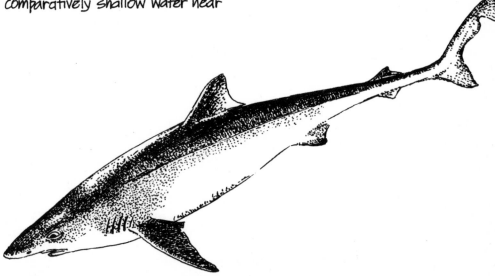

## TOPE

Shallow water is favoured by this small shark. It forms small packs and hunts small fish such as whiting and pouting. Bottom-living fish also form part of the diet, along with crustaceans. They are a sizeable fish, 50lb (23kg) or 60lb (27kg) not being uncommon.

# Species

BLUE SHARK

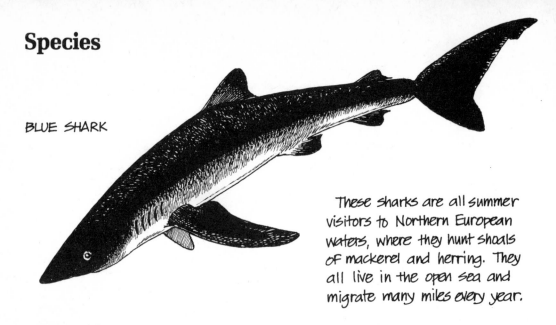

These sharks are all summer visitors to Northern European waters, where they hunt shoals of mackerel and herring. They all live in the open sea and migrate many miles every year.

THRESHER SHARK

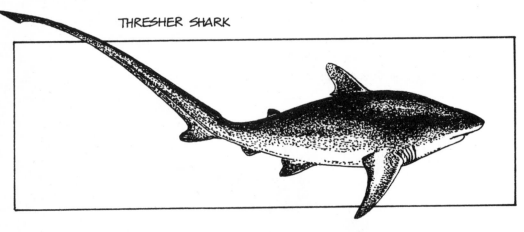

PORBEAGLE SHARK

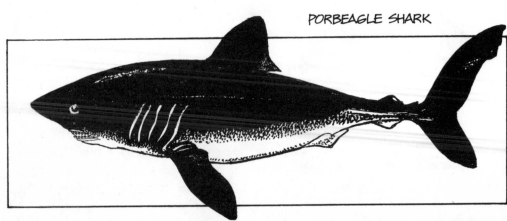

## CONGER AND LING

These two heavyweights live among the wrecks of ships, which are scattered over the seabed from the Bay of Biscay to the North Sea. The tangled hulks of sunken merchant and naval craft provide a haven for small fish, and this in turn presents easy pickings for these predators.

# Bait

## Crab

Peeler and softback crabs are the finest bait for most species of shore-caught fish. A crab is a peeler when it is in the process of losing its old shell. To test if a crab is a peeler, try lifting the rear end of the shell; it should come away easily.

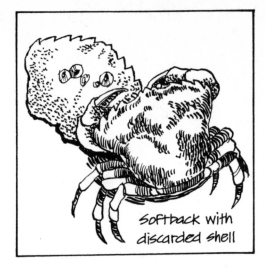

Softback with discarded shell

When a crab has discarded its old shell it is known as a softback. During this stage it is very vulnerable to attack, and can often be found hiding beneath a larger hardback. Both peelers and softbacks can be found beneath the weed on rocky foreshores. They will also bury themselves in mud.

To keep crabs alive and fresh, put them in a bucket or box, introduce some damp sea-weed and cover the container with an old towel which has been saturated in sea water. Store in a cool, dark place.

## Sandeel

This excellent bait can be collected from wet sand, where it lies buried on a receding tide, or purchased from the local seine-netters. They can be used as a dead bait, but are far more effective live.

To keep them alive, store them in a special bait bucket which has a battery-operated aerator to keep the water well oxygenated.

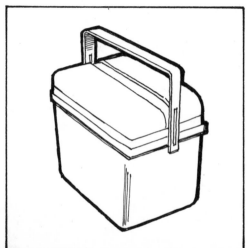

They will also survive in an ice box. Any surplus eels can be put into a freezer and used as dead-bait at a later date.

# Bait

## Lugworm

The lugworm lives in a 'U'-shaped burrow beneath the sand or mud. The colonies are exposed at low tide, and are evident by the casts.

Blow hole                    Cast

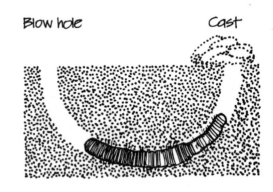

They can be kept fresh for a few days in sheets of newspaper, or for a longer period in fresh sea-water plus an aerator pump.

Dig with a broad-tined fork or a spade around the blow hole and the cast.

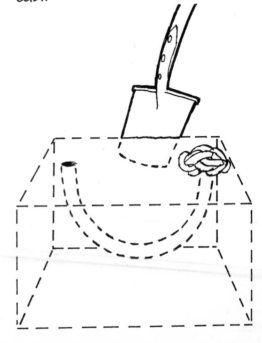

## Ragworm

There are three types of ragworm used for bait.

The king ragworm is huge: one of 12in (30cm) is by no means unusual. When handling these monsters, grip them immediately behind the head to prevent them turning and sinking their powerful pincers into your finger.

Harbour ragworm are very lively, reddish, and smaller than king ragworm. They are a good bait for dabs.

White ragworm are also lively little creatures, and provide a good bait for the mullet angler.

King ragworm live in a mixture of mud and shale. No small amount of physical exertion is required to extricate them with a fork. On occasions though, they can be exposed by simply lifting a rock.

The other two types of ragworm can be found on estuary mudflats at low tide, by digging with a fork or spade.

Ragworms are hardier than lugs and can be kept for a longer period. Check daily though, and discard any that are dead or mutilated.

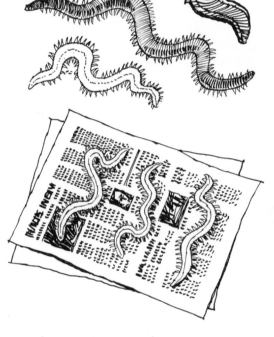

Store ragworms in newspaper or Vermiculite.

# Bait

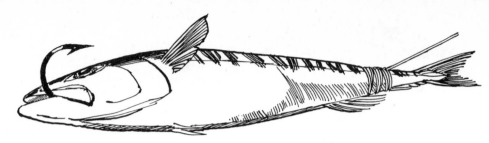

## Mackerel

This is an excellent bait for many sea fish, especially the deep-water species. There are various ways of presenting it on the hook.

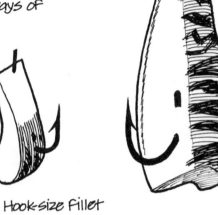

Whole side fillet

Chunk

Hook-size Fillet

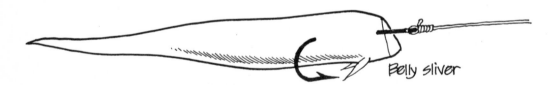

Belly sliver

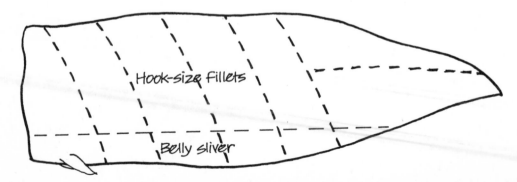

Hook-size Fillets

Belly sliver

# Squid

Like mackerel, squid can be mounted on the hook in various ways, to cater for different-sized fish.

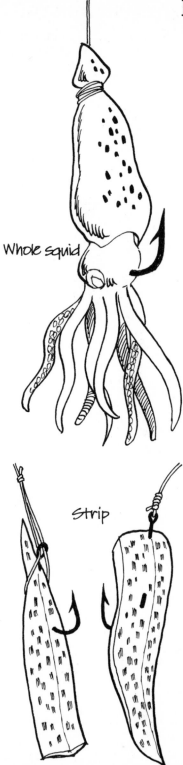

Whole squid

Body

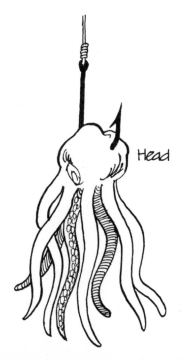

Head

Strip

# Bait presentation

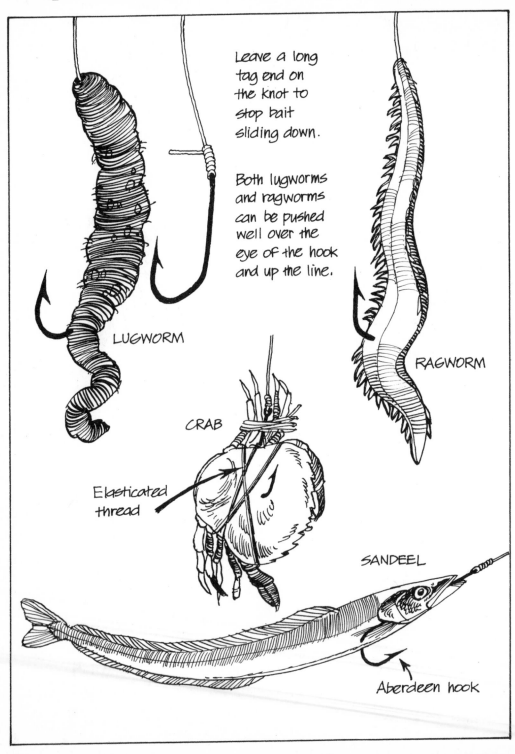

Leave a long tag end on the knot to stop bait sliding down.

Both lugworms and ragworms can be pushed well over the eye of the hook and up the line.

LUGWORM

RAGWORM

CRAB

Elasticated thread

SANDEEL

Aberdeen hook

# Bait clips

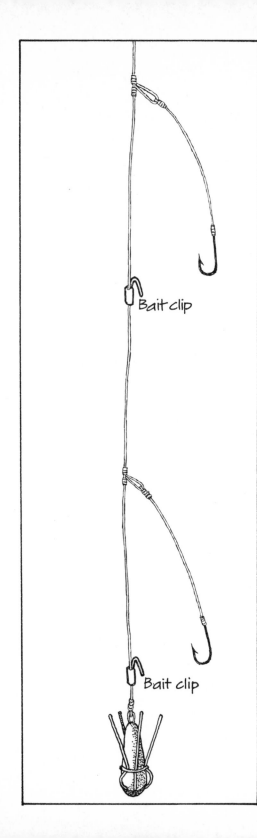

Bait clip

Bait clip

The clip is held in position by a short length of rubber tubing. Bait clips prevent tangles and cut down drag as the tackle flies through the air during a cast. This allows longer casts to be made. When the tackle hits the water, the hooks come free and the snoods resume their normal position.

A sliding stop knot above the hook prevents the bait from sliding too far up the line.

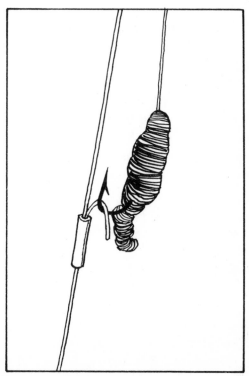

# Casting

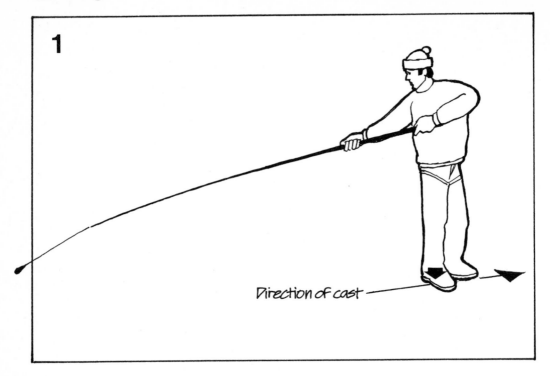

1

Direction of cast

## Basic off-the-ground cast

① Adopt a position with the left shoulder facing in the direction of the target. Turn to the right, and with the right arm fully extended, swing the lead back so that it is lying on the ground. Your weight should be on the right foot.

② Turn the head to look towards the target. Firmly, and smoothly, pull the rod up and forward, and at the same time swivel the body around to the left.

③ As the left arm straightens pull it down strongly and at the same time push forward with the right arm. All

the body-weight should now be on the left foot.

The basic off-the-ground cast is capable of producing casts of 100yd (91·5m) and more. Dirty, rough, steeply-shelving beaches, however, tend to reduce the efficiency of this cast. To overcome this problem the pendulum swing can be added, and this is shown overleaf.

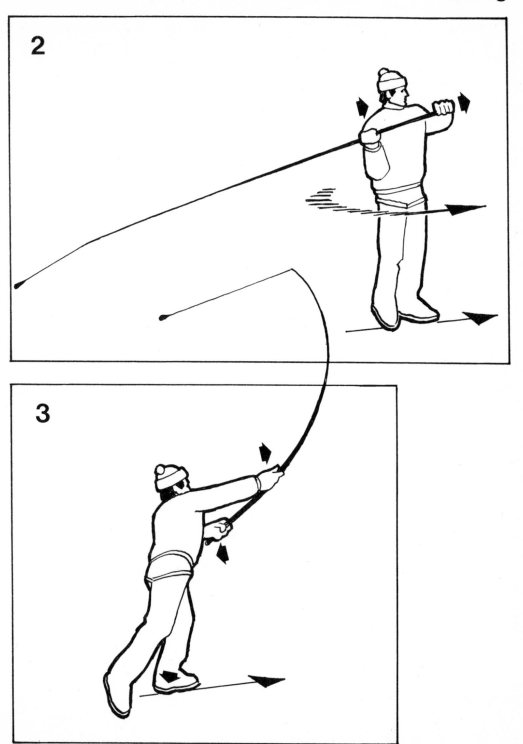

## Pendulum cast

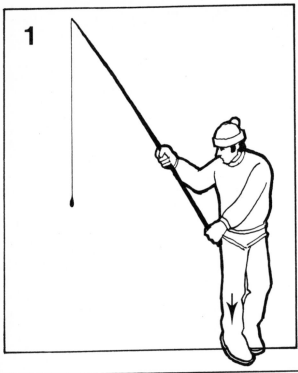

① Adopt the same position as for the off-the-ground cast, but this time hold the rod up, with about 6ft (1·85m) between tip and lead.

② Swing the lead to the left, then to the right.

③ At the top of the right hand swing, lower the rod to the second position of the off-the-ground cast.

④ The transition from one phase to another should be done smoothly to finish in the power-drive towards the target.

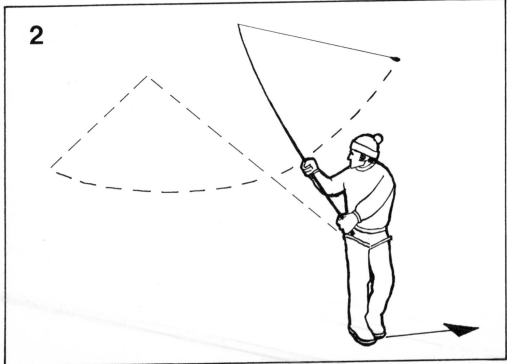

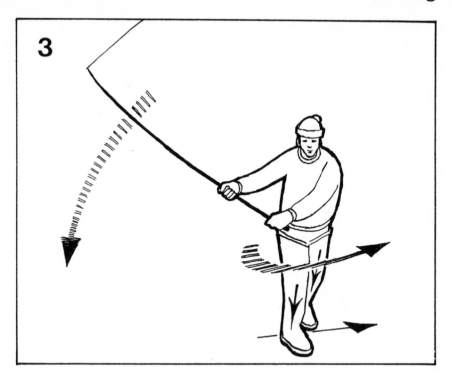

# Casting

The line release and follow-through is the same for both types of cast. As the lead passes the rod-tip, release line from the forefinger if using a fixed-spool, or the thumb if using a multiplier. Trap the line again as the lead hits the water. When the lead has sunk to the sea-bed, take up the slack line with a few turns of the reel handle.

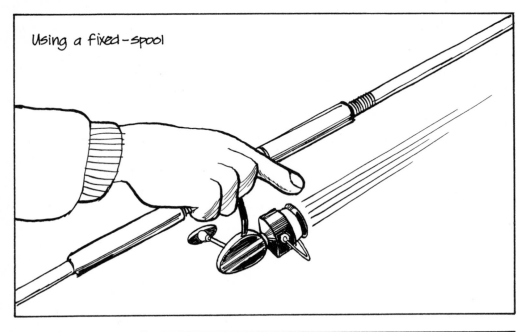

Using a fixed-spool

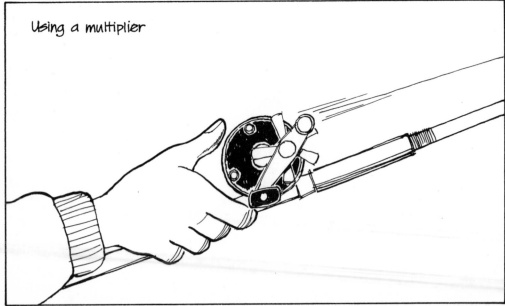

Using a multiplier

# After the cast

The rod can be held, which is preferable if the bites are coming with any frequency.

If bites are few and far between, it is better to prop the rod on a rest.

# Tides

Spring tides are high tides, and occur at new and full moon, when the gravitational pull of both sun and moon are in line with the earth.

Neap tides occur when the moon is in its first, or last, quarter and the gravitational influence of the moon is tempered by the pull of the sun.

Every serious sea-angler should possess a tide table. These are obtainable from fishing tackle shops or chandlers.

A knowledge of local tides is invaluable, not only for successful fishing, but also for productive bait collecting.

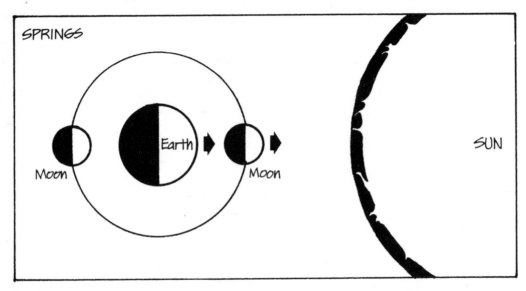

SPRINGS

Moon    Earth    Moon    SUN

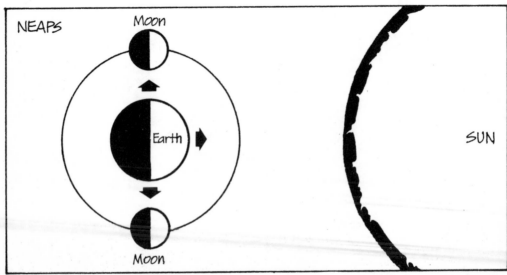

NEAPS

Moon    Earth    SUN    Moon

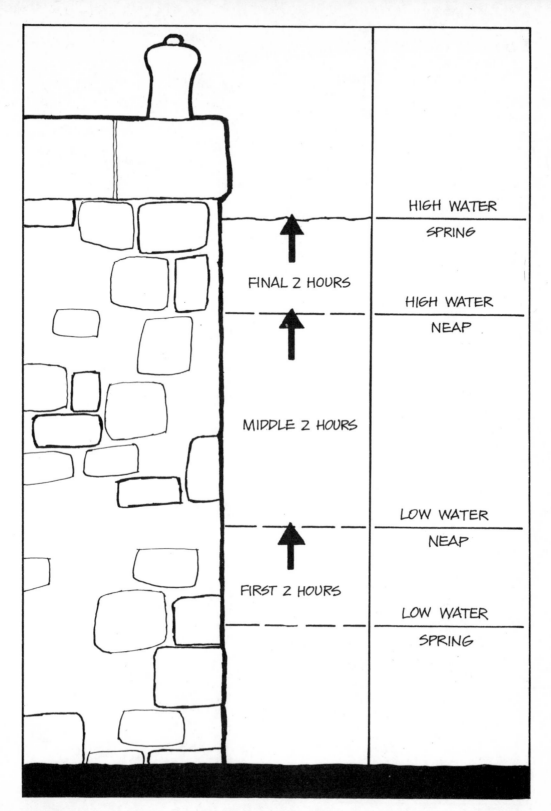

HIGH WATER
SPRING

FINAL 2 HOURS

HIGH WATER
NEAP

MIDDLE 2 HOURS

LOW WATER
NEAP

FIRST 2 HOURS

LOW WATER
SPRING

# Fishing from the shore

There are two distinct types of shore bass fishing: rock fishing, and fishing from a surf beach. Simplicity of tackle is the key to successful rock fishing.

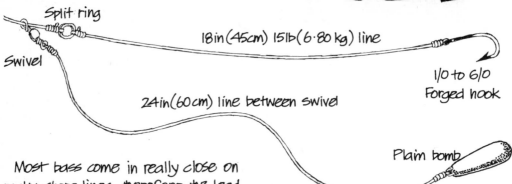

Split ring

Swivel

18in(45cm) 15lb(6·80 kg) line

24in(60cm) line between swivel

1/0 to 6/0
Forged hook

Plain bomb

Most bass come in really close on rocky shore-lines, therefore the lead does not need to be over 4oz (120g).

Rock bass like a big bait.

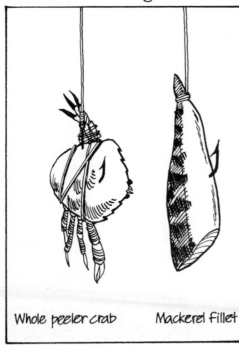

Whole peeler crab          Mackerel fillet

Hold the rod all the time; rock bass bite suddenly, and time wasted in grabbing a rod from a rest may well result in a lost fish, which will have gained the sanctuary of the rocks.

Fishing for bass in the surf of an Atlantic coast storm beach is quite different from the comparatively close-range approach of rock fishing. For a start, casts of 100yd (92·5m) and more are often necessary.

# Bass

The end rig is a little more sophisticated than that used for rock fishing, but still fairly basic.

Bait clip

24 in (60 cm) snood

'Breakaway' casting bomb

1/0 to 4/0 Fine wire Aberdeen hook

Start by casting your bait just beyond the third breaker. If there is no response, cast in to the flat area between you and the first breaker.

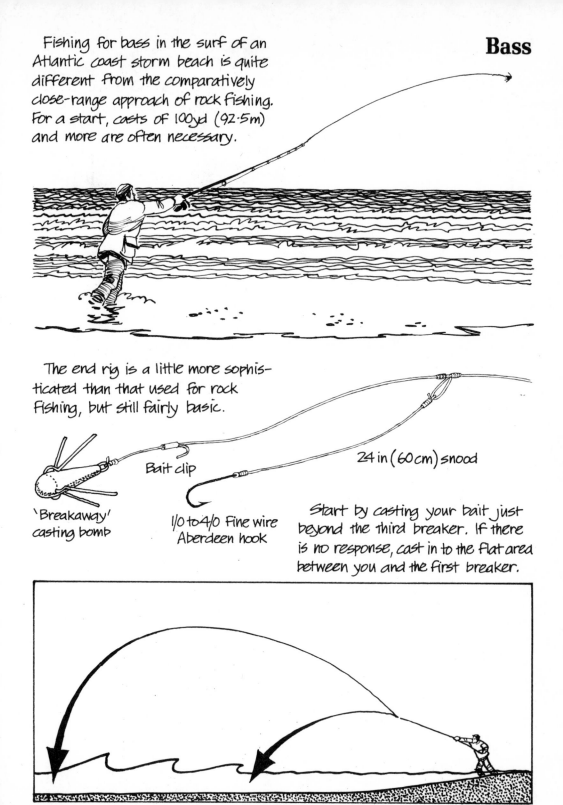

# Bass

Sandeel

Lugworm

Peeler crab

King ragworm

Baits for beach bass

Use the power of the breakers to help bring your bass towards the shore.

Wear a thick leather glove for lifting bass clear of the water to avoid injury from the fish's spines.

# Pollack

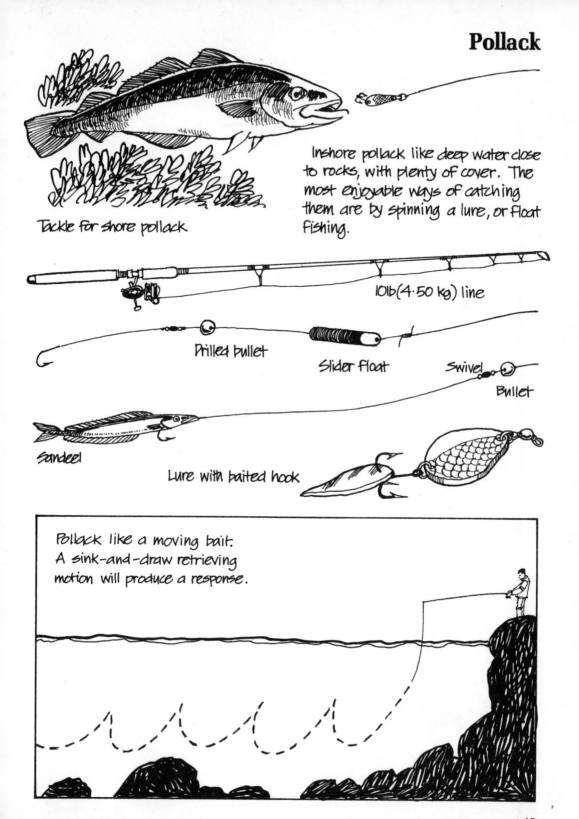

Inshore pollack like deep water close to rocks, with plenty of cover. The most enjoyable ways of catching them are by spinning a lure, or float fishing.

Tackle for shore pollack

10lb(4·50 kg) line

Drilled bullet

Slider float

Swivel

Bullet

Sandeel

Lure with baited hook

Pollack like a moving bait. A sink-and-draw retrieving motion will produce a response.

# Ballan wrasse

The best ballan wrasse fishing is found on the rocky Atlantic coastline.

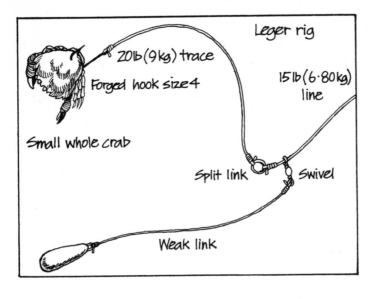

Leger rig

20lb (9kg) trace

Forged hook size 4

15lb (6·80kg) line

Small whole crab

Split link

Swivel

Weak link

It is best to use a long beachcaster rod for all types of wrasse fishing, as very often it will be necessary for the angler to apply pressure to a fish directly beneath his feet.

Bead

Stop knot

Slider float

10lb (4·50kg) line

Drilled bullet

Swivel

15lb (6·80kg) trace

Size 4 hook

This is the ideal fish for the novice. Whiting are ravenous and can be found anywhere during the winter.

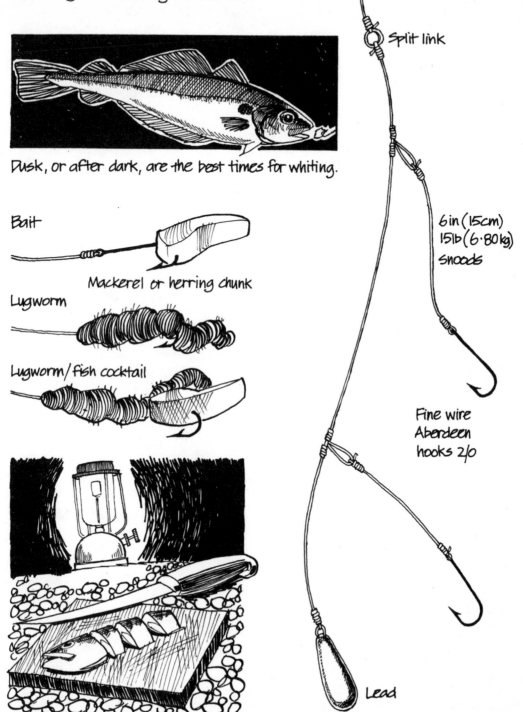

Dusk, or after dark, are the best times for whiting.

Bait

Mackerel or herring chunk

Lugworm

Lugworm / fish cocktail

Split link

6 in (15cm)
15lb (6.80kg)
snoods

Fine wire
Aberdeen
hooks 2/0

Lead

# Cod

Cod start to appear inshore during November, and become the main target for beachcasters throughout Britain and Northern Europe.

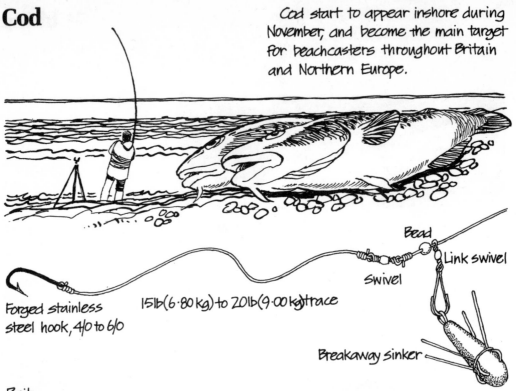

Forged stainless steel hook, 4/0 to 6/0

15lb (6·80 kg) to 20lb (9·00 kg) trace

Bead

Link swivel

Swivel

Breakaway sinker

## Bait

Cod will grab just about any bait, provided they are in a feeding mood. Here are a few worth trying.

Avoid cramming too much bait on the hook - leave the point and barb completely exposed.

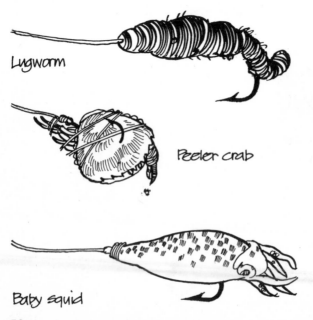

Lugworm

Peeler crab

Baby squid

During the winter, flounders can be caught in estuary systems throughout Britain and Europe.

# Flounder

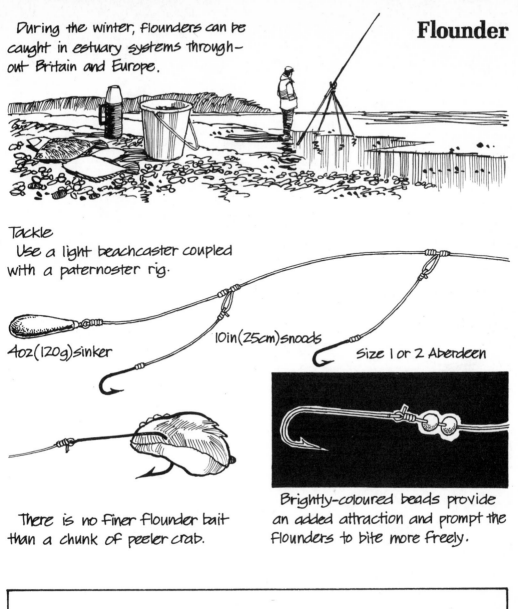

Tackle
Use a light beachcaster coupled with a paternoster rig.

4oz(120g)sinker

10in(25cm)snoods

Size 1 or 2 Aberdeen

There is no finer flounder bait than a chunk of peeler crab.

Brightly-coloured beads provide an added attraction and prompt the flounders to bite more freely.

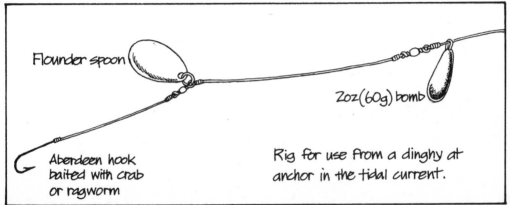

Flounder spoon

2oz(60g) bomb

Aberdeen hook baited with crab or ragworm

Rig for use from a dinghy at anchor in the tidal current.

# Dab

These are delightful little fish which, if you are fishing over the right ground, will supply plenty of bold bites, and provide a meal fit for a king.

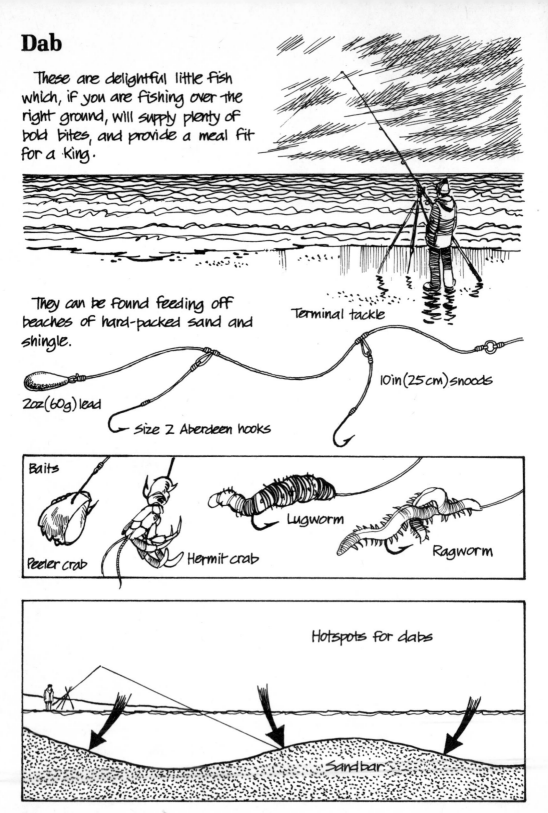

They can be found feeding off beaches of hard-packed sand and shingle.

Terminal tackle

2oz(60g) lead

Size 2 Aberdeen hooks

10in(25cm) snoods

Baits

Peeler crab

Hermit crab

Lugworm

Ragworm

Hotspots for dabs

Sandbar

# Dogfish

Lesser-spotted dogfish are a pest, but greater-spotted dogs (bull huss), and spur-dogs are well worth catching. They can be located off beaches that shelve quickly into deep water with a broken bottom.

Dogfish hunt in large packs, mopping up anything edible on or near the bottom.

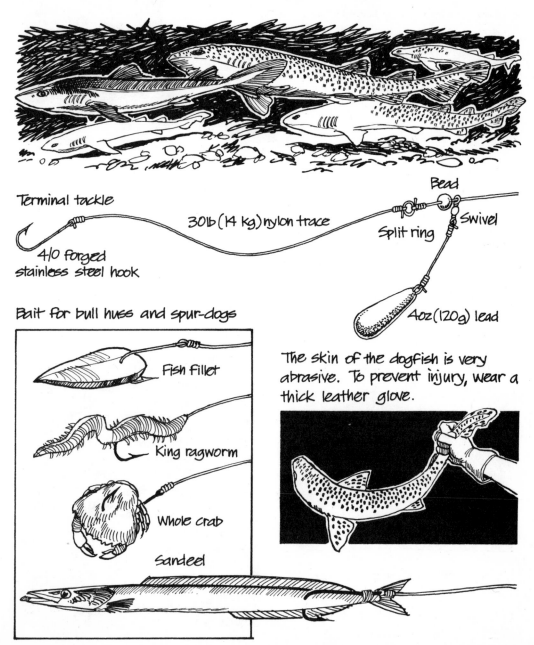

Terminal tackle

4/0 forged stainless steel hook

30 lb (14 kg) nylon trace

Bead

Split ring

Swivel

4 oz (120g) lead

Bait for bull huss and spur-dogs

Fish fillet

King ragworm

Whole crab

Sandeel

The skin of the dogfish is very abrasive. To prevent injury, wear a thick leather glove.

# Conger

To catch a conger from the shore look for a place with a good depth of water at low tide, and with plenty of rocks and weed on the bottom. Harbours immediately spring to mind, with walls built on a base of rocky ballast. Fish offal thrown from boats also provide the facilities for making harbours the number one choice for conger.

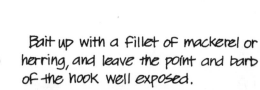

Swivel

Link swivel

Lead

18in (45cm) 100lb (45kg) cable-laid wire

6/0 seamaster or O'shaughnessy hook

A powerful beach rod and a multi-plier reel loaded with 30lb (14kg) line are necessary to pump congers clear of bottom snags.

Bait up with a fillet of mackerel or herring, and leave the point and barb of the hook well exposed.

# Tope

This fast-running fish can be caught from surf beaches, or from rock ledges bordering surf beaches.

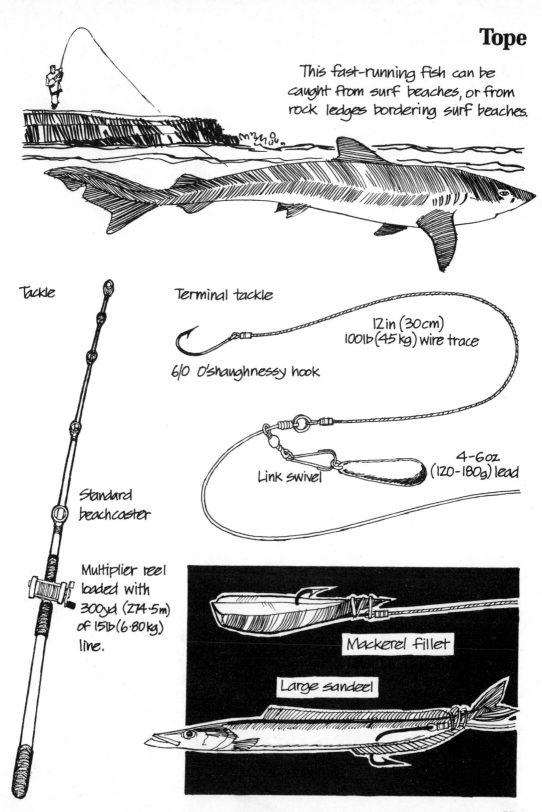

Tackle

Terminal tackle

12in (30cm) 100lb (45kg) wire trace

6/0 O'shaughnessy hook

Link swivel

4-6oz (120-180g) lead

Standard beachcaster

Multiplier reel loaded with 300yd (274.5m) of 15lb (6.80kg) line.

Mackerel fillet

Large sandeel

# Grey mullet

Contrary to popular belief, grey mullet can be caught regularly if the right approach is adopted.

Estuaries and harbours are their favourite haunts. Harbour mullet feed on a variety of scraps, eg., vegetable peelings, bacon rind, bread, rice and fish scraps. They can often be seen swimming beneath moored boats.

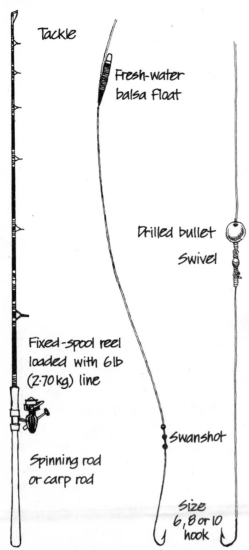

Tackle

Fresh-water balsa float

Drilled bullet

Swivel

Fixed-spool reel loaded with 6lb (2.70 kg) line

Swanshot

Spinning rod or carp rod

Size 6, 8 or 10 hook

A drop-net is absolutely essential for lifting large mullet up the side of a sheer harbour wall or pier.

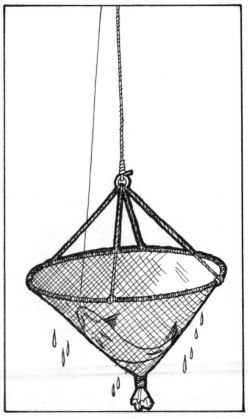

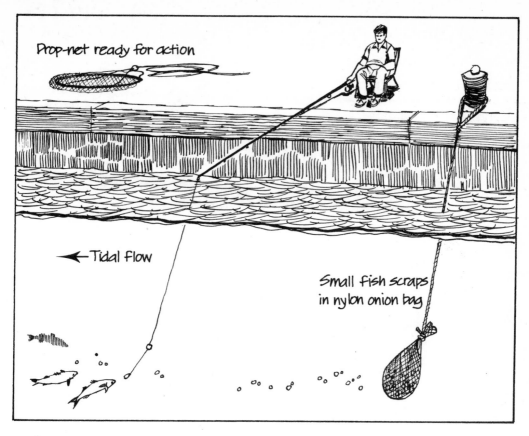

Prop-net ready for action

←Tidal flow

Small fish scraps in nylon onion bag

The secret of hooking mullet with this method is to wait until the rod tip is held down, then strike with a short movement of the wrist and forearm.

The best bait for harbour mullet is a small piece of mackerel flesh with skin attached.

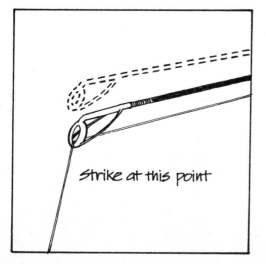

Strike at this point

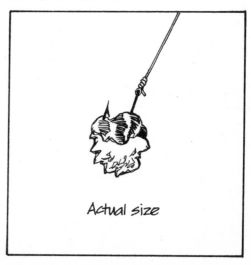

Actual size

# Mackerel

During the summer, mackerel shoals chase small fry close in to the shore, making it possible to present a bait on light tackle.

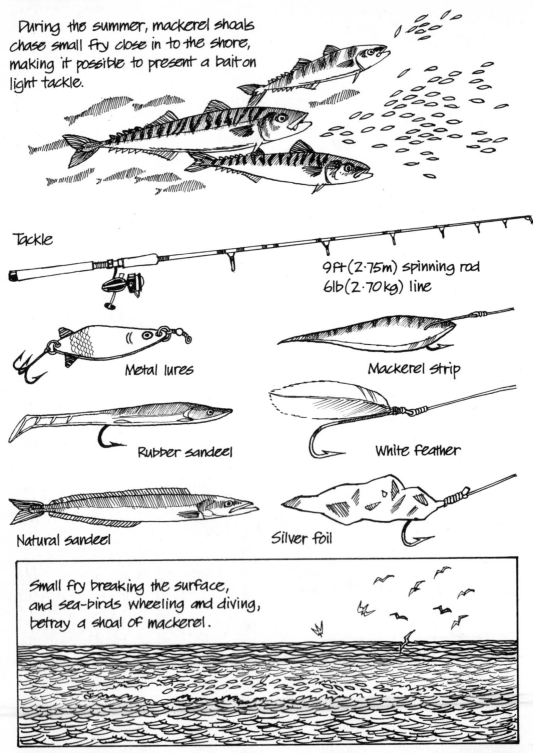

Tackle

9ft (2·75m) spinning rod
6lb (2·70kg) line

Metal lures

Mackerel strip

Rubber sandeel

White feather

Natural sandeel

Silver foil

Small fry breaking the surface, and sea-birds wheeling and diving, betray a shoal of mackerel.

Cast over and ahead of the fry disturbance and retrieve the lure with a sink-and-draw motion.

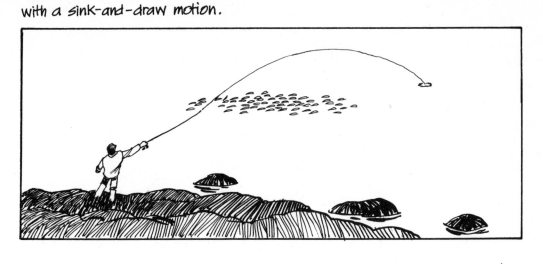

Anti-kink lead

Float tackle

Slider float

Stop knot

Garfish often swim with mackerel, and will respond to the same tactics. When hooked, they provide spectacular acrobatics.

Drilled bullet

Swivel

Mackerel strip

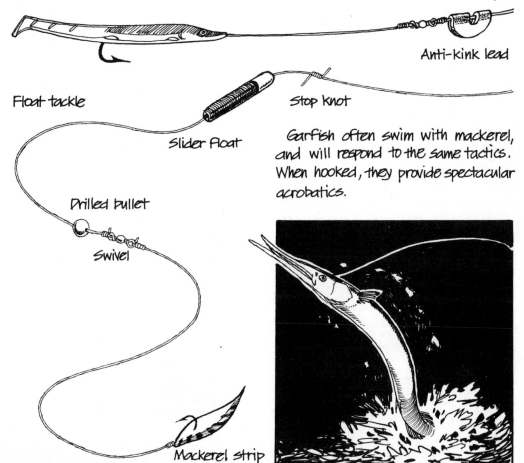

# Thornback and stingray

Thornback rays and stingrays can be taken on the same tackle, and by using the same tactics. Stingrays, however, do not arrive inshore as early as thornbacks, and should be expected when really warm weather prevails.

A warm summer evening, with a making tide, provides the ideal combination for contacting these two species.

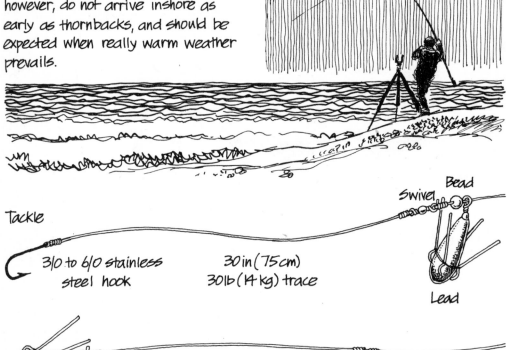

Tackle

3/0 to 6/0 stainless steel hook

30 in (75 cm)
30 lb (14 kg) trace

Swivel
Bead

Lead

30 in (75 cm) snood

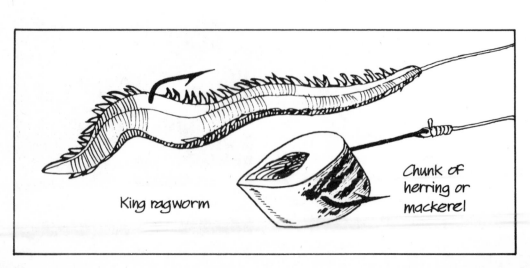

King ragworm

Chunk of herring or mackerel

# Boat fishing

Trolling is the practice of towing a natural or artificial lure 50 or 60yd (45m or 54m) astern of a slow-moving boat. The main species caught are bass and pollack.

Reefs and rocky shorelines provide the best locations for this method — probably the most famous in Europe is the Eddystone reef off the coasts of Devon and Cornwall.

Eddystone reef

A special rod will be required for trolling – something with a little more backbone than the one used for shore spinning and float work. An 'up-tide' rod fills the gap admirably.

A multiplier reel loaded with 25lb (11·50kg) line will complete the outfit.

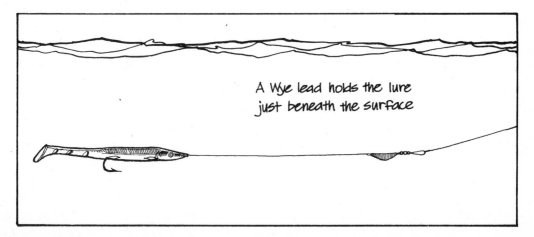

A Wye lead holds the lure just beneath the surface

# Inshore boat fishing

For a reasonable cost an inshore boat skipper will take a party of anglers up to three miles (5 km) out to sea.

An 8·8lb (4 kg) class rod will probably be sufficient to tackle most species encountered in inshore waters except, perhaps, tope and conger.

Much of this inshore fishing is done over rocky marks.

Light paternoster rigs are ideal for catching black and red bream, bass, whiting and cod.

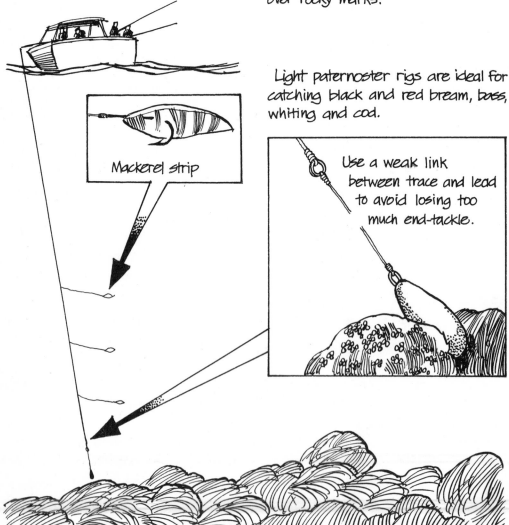

Mackerel strip

Use a weak link between trace and lead to avoid losing too much end-tackle.

# Driftlining

This form of fishing can be applied to most depths, but is more suited to medium and shallow areas. The boat is anchored up-tide of the mark, and the tackle is allowed to be carried on the tide towards the fish.

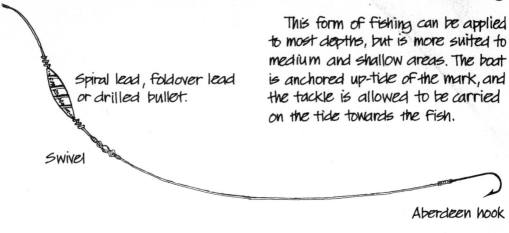

Spiral lead, foldover lead or drilled bullet.

Swivel

Aberdeen hook

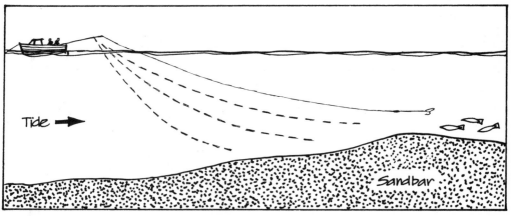

Tide →

Sandbar

This is an ideal method for taking bass that are feeding over a sand-bar in shallow water.

Live sandeel

# Fishing on the drift

This method is particularly effective for turbot and plaice. Providing the sea bed consists of clean sand, or shell grit (which it usually does where these species exist), it is possible to present the bait right on the bottom with leger tackle.

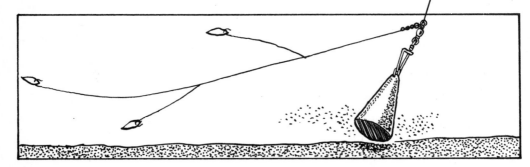

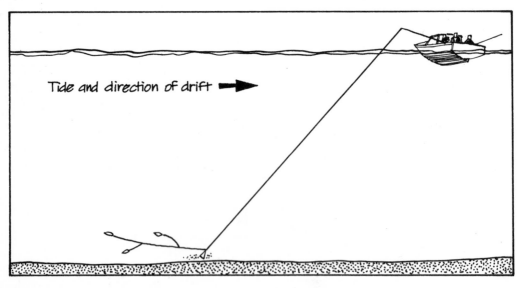

Tide and direction of drift ➡

Bait

Mackerel or sandeel strip

Hook size 1/0 to 6/0

# Legering

This method usually accounts for larger fish, so it is sensible to use a more robust rod. A 33lb (15kg) class rod will do, and this can also be used when fishing over a deep-water wreck.

A standard item of boat leger tackle is the Clement's boom, which keeps the trace away from the main line as the tackle is sinking.

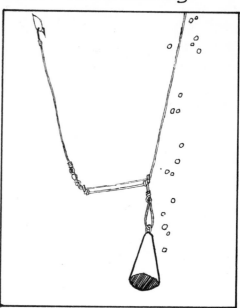

Rays respond well to this method of bait presentation.

Tope will require a longer than normal trace.

36 in (90 cm) nylon trace

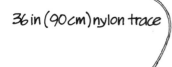

6/0 O'shaughnessy hook

12 in (30 cm) 100 lb (45 kg) wire trace

# Wreck fishing

Fishing over a deep-water wreck will require a bigger financial outlay than inshore fishing, but will produce larger than average specimens. 30lb (14 kg) line will be needed, coupled with a 33lb (15 kg) class rod.

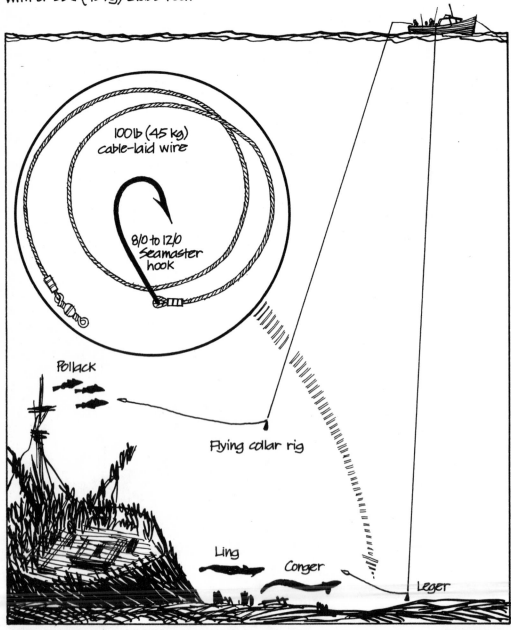

100lb (45 kg) cable-laid wire

8/0 to 12/0 Seamaster hook

Pollack

Flying collar rig

Ling

Conger

Leger

# Wreck fishing

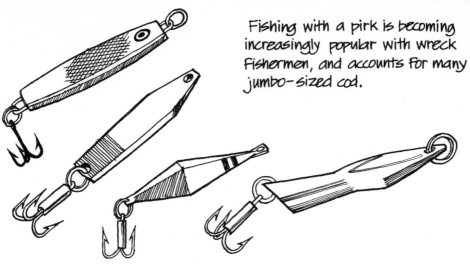

Fishing with a pirk is becoming increasingly popular with wreck fishermen, and accounts for many jumbo-sized cod.

The pirk is lowered to the required depth, then worked up and down by raising and lowering the rod. This produces an attractive, fluttering action which is irresistible to big predators.

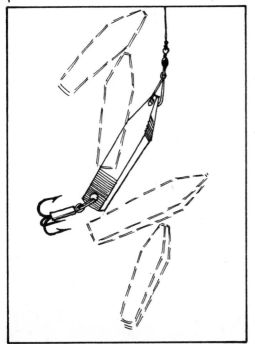

Variation on a pirk theme.

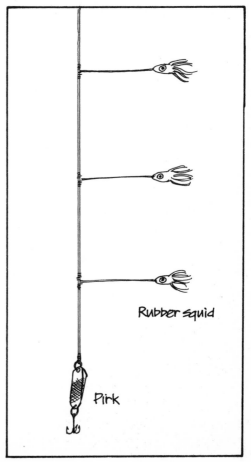

Rubber squid

Pirk

# Shark fishing

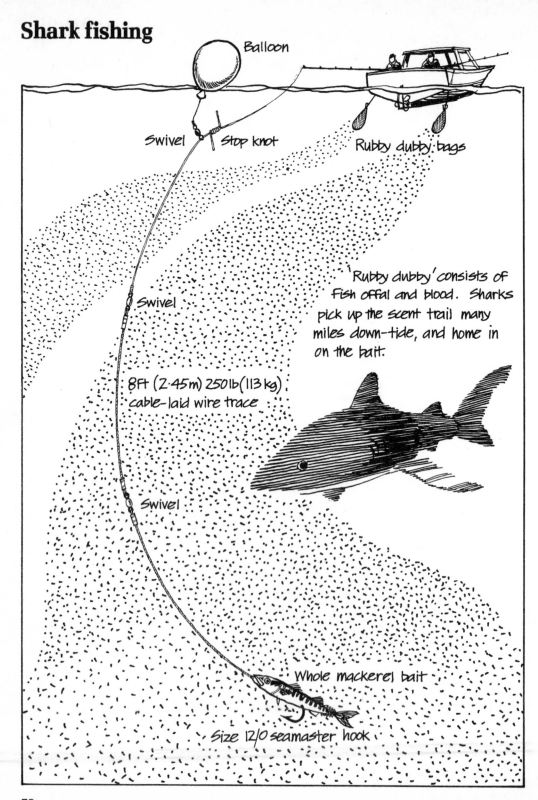

Balloon

Swivel   Stop knot

Rubby dubby bags

'Rubby dubby' consists of
fish offal and blood. Sharks
pick up the scent trail many
miles down-tide, and home in
on the bait.

Swivel

8ft (2·45m) 250lb (113kg)
cable-laid wire trace

Swivel

Whole mackerel bait

Size 12/0 seamaster hook

# Playing a fish

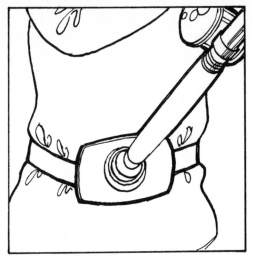

Bringing a heavy fish up through several fathoms of water puts a strain on both angler and tackle.

To protect the angler's groin, a special butt pad is worn.

With the brake on the reel in the 'on' position, and the drag set to the highest possible tension, subject to the breaking strain of the line, the rod is lifted hard into the fish.

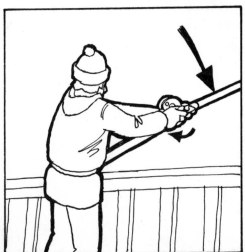

The rod is then lowered, and at the same time line is retrieved onto the spool.

Once again the rod is lifted, and the same operation is repeated until the fish arrives at the surface.

# Clothing

Even in summer it can feel cold onboard a boat. This can be miserable, and definitely affects concentration and efficient angling.

Exposed beaches can be the most soul-destroying places if you are not equipped with sufficient clothing. You can always shed clothing if you become too warm. You cannot conjure up extra layers when you have not taken enough.

ITEMS

Boat angler— woolly hat, polo-neck sweater, pvc jacket with hood, waterproof over-trousers, rope-soled yachting shoes.

Beach angler— woolly hat, polo-neck sweater, waxed or pvc jacket and hood, waders.

Boat angler

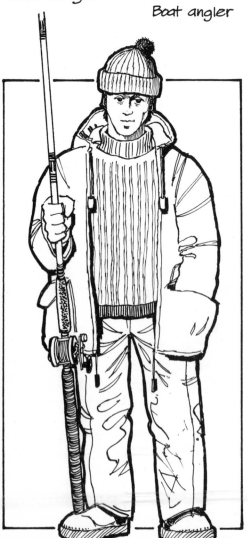

Beach angler

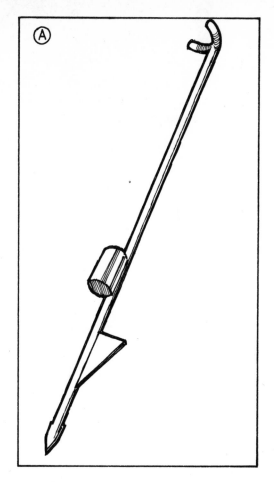

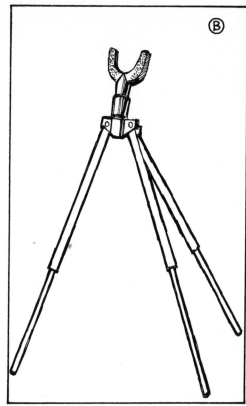

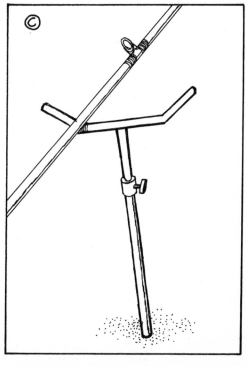

# Rod rests

Ⓐ The monopod is ideal in firm sand and mud, but is not suited to hard surfaces and very large pebbles.

Ⓑ The tripod, however, will cope with most surfaces and is probably the most sensible choice for the newcomer.

Ⓒ This very basic but useful rest is popular with many top beach anglers. It allows the rod to be propped at a variety of angles.

# Accessories

## KNIFE
This is an essential piece of equipment both for filleting fish and for cutting up fish and crab baits. It should be kept razor-sharp at all times.

## TACKLE BOX
For containing small items of tackle in an orderly fashion. Most boxes nowadays are plastic, which is non-corrosive, but the fittings are metal and will need to be treated every so often with water repellant spray and oil.

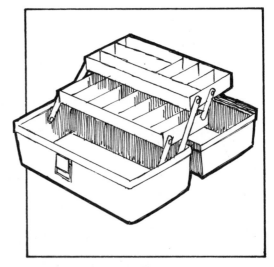

## PRESSURE LAMP
There are quite a few different types to choose from. They all provide a good light, necessary for beach fishing after dark, and a source of heat for cold fingers.

HOOK SHARPENING STONE
When fishing over rough ground, hooks are liable to lose their sharpness very quickly. Check the hook before every cast, and if it is blunt use the stone. If the hook is damaged, tie on a new one.

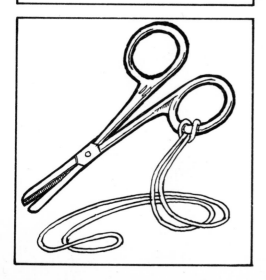

UMBRELLA
This piece of equipment is usually associated with the fresh-water fishing scene, but is just as necessary on a wet and windswept beach, for keeping the angler and his equipment dry.

ARTERY FORCEPS
When buying forceps for sea fishing, make sure that they are made from stainless steel. Keep them close at hand for extracting hooks from fish. The best way to do this is to fasten them to a lanyard and hang them around your neck.

# Knots

## TUCKED FULL BLOOD KNOT

For joining line of widely-differing thickness. The thinner line must be doubled at the tying end, and taken around the thicker line twice as many times as the thicker line is turned around it.

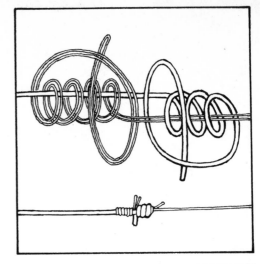

## PALOMAR KNOT

A simple, neat and efficient knot for connecting a hook to nylon line.

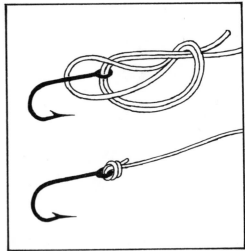

## UNI KNOT

One of the strongest knots in use today. This is another good knot for connecting lead to a shock leader. It is also very popular among deep-sea anglers.

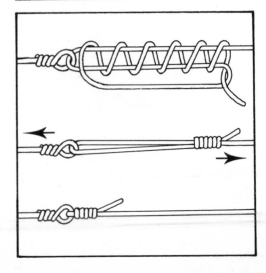

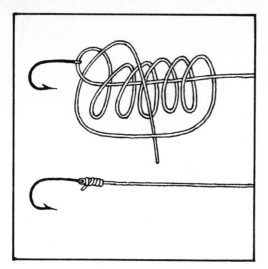

### TUCKED HALF-BLOOD KNOT

For joining hooks, swivels and leads to line. Properly tied, this is a safe knot for joining a sinker to the end of a shock leader. Serious injuries have been inflicted by leads flying off during the cast. Frequently check the knot joining lead to leader.

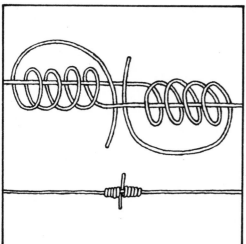

### FULL BLOOD KNOT

The best knot for joining two lengths of line of the same, or similar, thickness.

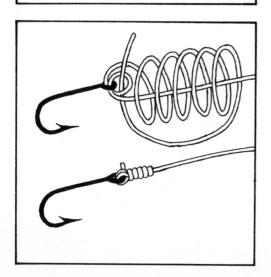

### CLINCHED HALF-BLOOD KNOT

A better knot for use on heavier—gauged hooks.

**DROPPER LOOP KNOT**
The only knot for creating a connecting point for paternoster snoods.

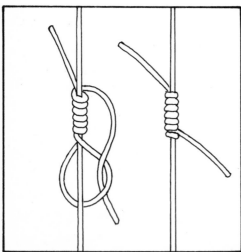

**STOP KNOT**
A very useful knot when fishing with a sliding float. Leave both tag ends very long for maximum efficiency.

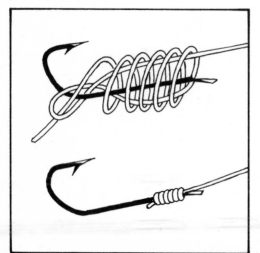

**SPADE-END KNOT**
Mainly used for making up a team of mackerel feathers.

# Remember!

Salt water causes corrosion to metal surfaces. Reels and rod fittings both contain metal, and both items are expensive. After every fishing session, wash rod and reel under cold, fresh water.

Spray reels with water repellant, and oil and grease necessary points.

Every so often, strip reels down completely and clean the internal mechanism, re-grease and re-assemble.

By following this simple procedure your reel will last a lifetime and function efficiently to give you trouble-free fishing.